# MY LITTLE PONY COLLECTIBLES

Ilona Iske and Ossie from MLPMerch

AMBERLEY

First published 2018

Amberley Publishing
The Hill, Stroud
Gloucestershire, GL5 4EP

www.amberley-books.com



ISBN 978 1 4456 8342 3 (print)
ISBN 978 1 4456 8343 0 (ebook)



British Library Cataloguing in Publication Data.
A catalogue record for this book is available from the British Library.

Origination by Amberley Publishing.
Printed in the UK.

# Contents

# Preface

We're incredibly proud to present this book to you. Our first published work outside of our blog MLPMerch.com was quite an experience, and we're happy that you've decided to pick it up. Our intention for this book is to not make a physical version of our *My Little Pony* database, but to extend on that. You won't find every pony ever released in this book – far from it – but you will find interesting stories and fascinating ponies that make collecting fun. You'll read about the very first pony, which wasn't even named *My Little Pony*, shipments full of broken pony figures and incredibly hard to find ponies. We've tried our best to put every pony with a story into this book, along with an introduction for collectors that are relatively new to the world of *My Little Pony*.

We, as fellow collectors, hope that you enjoy *My Little Pony Collectibles* and are inspired to start, or continue, your *My Little Pony* collection.

Ilona and Ossie

# Introduction

The history starts with Bonnie Zacherle, who officially invented the toy that started *My Little Pony*. During the mid-1970s she started with several freelance jobs for Hasbro. In 1980 she joined Hasbro's Research and Development Illustration team, where she could work on new concepts for the company.[1] Inspired by her childhood dream of owning a pony, together with sculptor Charles Muenchinger a design and patent were made for a 10-inch-tall brown toy pony figure.[2] This concept was accepted by Hasbro and marketed as 'My Pretty Pony'. Shortly afterwards, two more releases of My Pretty Pony were produced – one pink variant that introduced the idea of symbols (or cutie marks) and another release of the brown pony combined with a smaller pony called Beautiful Baby.

In 1982 Hasbro decided to continue the line under the name *My Little Pony*, featuring downsized pony figures, colourful designs and more symbols. Although the first sets were available in 1982, Hasbro themselves stick to 1983 as the start of *My Little Pony*. This first official *My Little Pony* generation continued until 1992 in the United States and 1995 overseas.

After a short break Hasbro revived the *My Little Pony* series in 1997 with the launch of *Friendship Garden*, or Generation 2, with renewed figure designs. The second generation only lasted two years in the United States, but more figures were released in several countries in Europe due to their popularity. In 2003 the last figures were developed for the European market because of the global launch of a new *My Little Pony* generation.

This third series, which launched in 2003, featured yet another style of pony figures and ran until 2009. In 2008 a small reboot, usually referred to as Generation 3.5, reduced the amount of characters down to seven and introduced the concept of blind bags.

Starting in 2010, *My Little Pony: Friendship is Magic* is the current generation of *My Little Pony* figures. This line is closely tied with the identically named television show, following character releases and storylines. Up until today the series has seen various side lines, like Equestria Girls and Guardians of Harmony, as well as an overall design change in 2017.

All the different generations of ponies next to each other.

# Collecting *My Little Pony*

## The Basics

Not every collector is the same; some prefer to get everything in packaging, others only want one certain pony or generation and so on. It's up to you what kind of collector you want to be when you decide to collect *My Little Pony*.

The first key concept is the difference between each generation. You can identify the generations in various ways. Each generation is different to the next so it shouldn't be that hard to see which generation you're dealing with. We've written down some of the most recognisable features of each generation:

**Generation 1:**
- Material is a soft vinyl plastic that you can squeeze without much pressure.
- The normal-sized ponies are about 5 inches tall.

**Generation 2:**
- More slender and realistically shaped than G1.
- Feathered hooves.
- Eyes have gems inside of them.

**Generation 3:**
- Chubbier bodies, much like G1.
- Their bodies are made of a harder vinyl than G1.
- Some will have a pearlescent-effect body and magnets underneath them.

**Generation 3.5:**
- Made of the same material as G3.
- Body shape is more cartoon-styled, with larger heads than normal. They are also a tad smaller than G3.

**Generation 4:**
- Smaller than older generations, at about 3 inches for a regular release. There are also releases where the pony is about 6 or 8 inches tall.
- Very stylised in terms of shape compared to the other generation.

The condition of the pony is perhaps one of the most important things to look at when buying a pony as it determines the value. The better the condition, the more valuable a pony can be. Things like tangled hair can be fixed quickly with the use of shampoo and conditioner and several markings can be removed easily with some acetone, or sometimes just a little bit of soap. There are plenty of guides online available to help you in restoring your pony. However, it can be wise to keep your pony as much in the original state as possible. Sometimes when the hair is just too far gone people can decide to replace it with new hair. While sometimes the difference can't be seen, some people prefer the original hair over better, non-original hair.

Aside from the pony itself, the completeness of the set also counts towards the value. Most ponies originally came with accessories like outfits, combs or pets. Getting a full set of accessories for older ponies can be quite a challenge, and every collector handles this differently. Some prefer a complete set for each pony, while others only collect the figures and see any accessories as a nice but optional bonus. If you prefer to hunt down accessories, be aware that the combined sum for all the parts might be more than the cost of the pony itself!

As for displaying, cabinets or shelves are a good option, but make sure that the room isn't too moist, and it's also best to avoid placing them in direct sunlight as it will damage the body. This counts for packaged ponies too, as the cardboard can get affected by water and the plastic can discolour or crack after too much exposure to sunlight.

A way to display your collection is by using glass cabinets.

## Terms of the Trade

Looking online for new ponies to add to your collection and getting dizzy from all the terms and abbreviations? We've collected the most common terms used between *My Little Pony* collectors to help you understand the language.

| | |
|---|---|
| Bait | A pony figure beyond repair, usually bought for a low price and used for customizing the figure. |
| CM | Cutie Mark – The little icon on the pony's flank, indicating his/her talent in the world of *My Little Pony: Friendship is Magic* and that of Generation 3. For the other generations see Symbol, below. |
| EqG/EG | Equestria Girls – A spin-off of the *My Little Pony* franchise featuring the main characters from *My Little Pony: Friendship is Magic* as human high school students. |
| Fakie | A fake *My Little Pony* figure, either being a direct bootleg figure or purposely created look-a-likes in the *My Little Pony* style. |
| FiM | *Friendship is Magic* – The name of the fourth-generation *My Little Pony* television show. |
| G1/G2/G3/G3.5/G4 | The different generations of *My Little Pony.* |
| MIB | Mint in Box – Figures still inside the original box and of superior quality. |
| MLP | Short for *My Little Pony.* |
| MOC | Mint on Card(board) – Figures still placed on the original cardboard packaging and of superior quality. |
| OOAK | One of a Kind – A term most frequently used for customised figures that are hand-crafted and not produced in bulk. |
| SDCC | San Diego Comic Con – A large comic, entertainment and pop culture convention in San Diego, California, where Hasbro and partners frequently sell exclusive merchandise. |
| Symbol | The icon on the flank of the pony. This goes for Generation 1 and 2; for the G3+ term see Cutie Mark. |
| TAF | Twice as Fancy – A line of G1 ponies that have larger symbols that commonly cover the complete flanks. They sometimes have smaller symbols on their face too. |

## Determining Prices

The only moment *My Little Pony* figures have a set price range is when they're still on the shelves at official retailers. As soon as the stores have refreshed their stock, or the ponies are simply sold out, prices are affected by supply and demand in the collectors' community and online merchants. Ponies from older generations and hard to find figures can go for prices far above their original retail value, while factors like packaging, damage and accessories can further influence the price of a specific figure.

For collectors looking to expand their collection, it's key to know what a certain pony is worth. One common way to research prices is to check online marketplaces like eBay. It is important to note that you should not only check the prices of active listings, but also those of already sold figures (if available); it might be that list prices are far higher than what collectors are actually willing to pay.

Aside from direct price information, marketplaces also give you an insight in how the balance between supply and demand is. A lot of listings for a certain pony, but no actual sales? This marks an overload of supply or lack of demand, which usually results in a price drop. Does a certain pony sell within hours after being listed? This is a result of high demand or low supply, commonly followed by increased prices.

Another way to get a general idea of what a pony is worth is by asking the community. Online there are plenty of community-driven forums that focus on collecting (older generation) *My Little Pony* figures and merchandise, and within these communities you'll often find discussions about prices, price requests and ponies for sale, all by fellow collectors. And, if a certain pony has no pricing information available, you can always post your own question on one of these forums for help.

Even with these steps to determine prices, there are a few tips you might want to follow before you buy a pony for your collection:

- Mind your budget; collecting is fun, but it shouldn't put you in financial trouble.
- Do your homework; don't go for the first listing or price suggestion you see, try to find multiple source of information.
- Check the state; ponies that are still in their original packaging are way more expensive than loose figures without accessories. When doing your research, try to find prices of comparable figures.

## Identifying Bootlegs

If a toy line is popular, it's common to see unofficial figures following, trying to cash in on the success of said line. Ever since the first generation of *My Little Pony* fakes have been produced, often referred by the community as 'Fakies'. While that is a sweet name, bootleg pony figures are usually of a lesser quality and are not endorsed or licensed by Hasbro.

To avoid getting duped by a bootlegged figure, knowing how to identify fake ponies is key. There's a high chance a pony is fake when:

- It doesn't mention Hasbro anywhere.
- The packaging does not explicitly say '*My Little Pony*'.
- The quality is much lower than normal ponies; look out for badly rooted hair, a bad paint job or very thin plastic.
- They have a different mould, which doesn't resemble any of the released ponies by Hasbro under the *My Little Pony* line.

If you are uncertain if your pony is official or not, feel free to ask the community! Ironically enough, several Fakies are actually highly sought after!

Fake My Little Pony figures can come in copied, modified or unique moulds.

# Generation 0

**My Pretty Pony**
**Release year: 1981**

Although not part of the official *My Little Pony* line, the My Pretty Pony was quite important for the history of the ponies we're all familiar with now. You might even say that this one is the grandmother of all the current ponies.

Under her chin is a small button, which, when pressed, will cause the pony to blink and move her ears. She also came with several accessories like a hat, saddle, ribbons and a pattern to create custom blankets for her.

Two versions were released, the first being of a brown pony with blonde hair and the second one, a pink variant, was pretty similar to the pony we now know as Peachy from the first generation of *My Little Pony*. The brown pony saw another release later on in a combination with a smaller yellow pony known as the My Pretty Pony and Beautiful Baby set.[3]

The My Pretty Pony.

# Generation 1

Generation 1 is officially the start of the *My Little Pony* line. The first set contained ponies with the exact same pose, which was very similar to My Pretty Pony. Quickly after the series evolved, with more moulds, gimmicks and pony variants. Many of these choices form the base for many *My Little Pony* figures to come, including all other generations – what would a *My Little Pony* be without a symbol on its hip?

The release year of the first generation is commonly counted with 1982/83 as the first year, which is referred to by collectors as 'Year One'. In this book we'll follow this way of counting, but we'll include the actual years of release too.

Generation 1 Bubbles (left), Chatterbox (top) and Baby Star Flower (below).

## Highlights of Ponies and Sets

**Flat-Footed Collector Ponies**
**Release year: Year One (1982–83)**
**Set: Year One Collector Ponies**

*My Little Pony* officially started in 1982 with the release of six ponies all sharing the same pose, which was later called the 'Collectors Pose'. In contrast with most other Generation 1 ponies, the first set all have flat feet, whereas newer ponies got an inner curve (or concave) under their feet.

The classic six 'Flat-Footed' ponies are Blossom, Blue Belle, Butterscotch, Cotton Candy, Minty and Snuzzle. Because these six are the first ponies under the *My Little Pony* brand, they've been re-released for special occasions, such as the 25th anniversary in 2008 and the 35th anniversary in 2018.

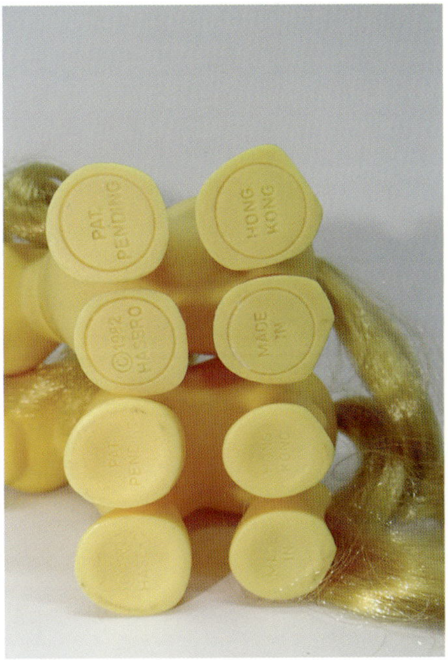

*Above left*: Here you can see the difference between the two types of feet.

*Above right*: The 35th anniversary re-release of Cotton Candy. (Photograph by Linda van Leeuwen)

*Right*: The 25th anniversary re-releases of Blue Belle, Butterscotch and Cotton Candy. (Photograph by Linda van Leeuwen)

Flat-Footed Butterscotch.

**Sea Ponies**
**Release year: Year Two to Six (1983–88)**

Who said that ponies could only live on land? In Year Two people were first introduced to the Sea Ponies. In terms of designs they resemble actual seahorses, having fins instead of legs. The adult versions came with shells, which you could stick to bathroom walls, and the baby versions came with floaties to help them float. They also have a weight inside them to make them float more 'naturally'. The downside to this is that if the pony has been in contact with water a lot the weight could rust and eventually cover the inside of the pony with mould.

*Above left*: Seaspray is a European exclusive Sea Pony.

*Above right*: Surf Rider the Baby Sea Pony (left) and Beachcomber the Pretty and Pearly Baby Sea Pony (right), both with float.

Baby Ribbon (left) and Baby Gusty (right), the Beddy Bye Eye Ponies.

**Beddy Bye Eye Ponies**
**Release year: Year Three and Four (1984–86)**

Year Three saw the release of the first Beddy Bye Eye Ponies, also known as BBE Ponies. These baby ponies had a gimmick that when you lie the pony down on its side, the eyes would close. While the idea sounds kind of cute, the execution wasn't that great, and the ponies would often look very creepy. What's even worse is that the sockets of the eyes are made of metal, which is prone to rusting, making the poor pony look even creepier! Because of this some people like to remove the eyes, fill the holes and paint the regular printed eyes over it.

**Twinkle Eye Ponies**
**Release year: Year Four and Five (1985–87)**

Twinkle Eye Ponies look just like your average G1 pony from a distance, though there's one major difference visible on their faces – their eyes are jewels. The *My Little Pony* comic *Applejack's Amazing Adventure* explains how they got their eyes. According to the story there was an evil Jewel Wizard who had ponies work in a cave to smash up rocks and gather jewels. They had been working in the cave for such a long time that their eyes could no longer bear the daylight. In the end Applejack smashed his throne and jewels flew everywhere, with the wizard falling into an abyss below. Some of the throne's jewels flew into the eyes of the worker ponies, returning their vision.

Two sets were released during the G1 period; the first set in Year Four, which included a total of nine ponies, and a second set of five more ponies in Year Five. There was also a Party Pack, which also included a Twinkle Eye Pony named Party Time.

However, there's one Twinkle Eye Pony who seems to be the most popular – Mimic. She was released in Year Five as part of the second set together with Bright Eyes, Locket, Quackers and Tic Tac Toe. Due to unknown circumstances her production amount was lower than that of the other ponies. This, in combination with her quite unusual colour scheme, makes her a very sought after pony for collectors and one of the more expensive worldwide released G1 Ponies.

Whizzer, the Year Four Twinkle-Eyed Pony.

Mimic, the Year Five Twinkle-Eyed Pony. (Photograph by K. Bollmeier)

Twilight, the Year Five So-Soft Pony.

**So Soft Ponies**
**Release year: Year Four and Five (1985–87)**

Regular ponies' hair might be real, but their body remains vinyl, so it isn't that great to snuggle with, right? In Year Four we got to meet the So Soft Ponies, with bodies completely covered with flocking, making them feel really soft. A total of thirty So Soft Ponies have been released, divided over two sets and several other releases as well. When it comes to restoring So-Soft Ponies, it's possible that sometimes the flocking is in such a bad state that collectors decide to de-flock them. What's then left is a regular looking G1 pony, but they can still look very pretty! In the UK some of them were even released without their flocking.[4]

**Flutter and Winger Ponies**
**Release year: Year Four to Seven (1985–89)**

In Year Four we got to meet a new species of ponies – the Flutter Ponies. These were ponies who were smaller and more slender than regular ponies, but their biggest feature was their wings. If you gently pressed the button on their back, their wings would move up and down. There was, however, one big downside to these ponies: their wings were extremely fragile and got lost or broke off quickly. Because of that a Flutter Pony with intact wings is worth a lot more than one without. Over the years reproduction wings have been made by collectors that are almost an exact match to the original ones, but there are also people who like to create totally new kinds of wings with lots of details. One thing can be said for sure: no one likes a Flutter Pony without wings.

But Flutter Ponies aren't the only ponies with bug-like wings. In Year Six Hasbro introduced the Summerwing Ponies and in Year Seven the Windy Wing Ponies. They are often named Flitter or Winger Ponies. They are smaller than the Flutter Ponies with wings that are sturdier and include multiple colours and patterns like butterflies.

*Left*: Wingsong, the Year Five Flutter Pony with accurate reproduction wings.

*Below*: High Flier, the Summer Wing Pony (left), and Cool Breeze (right), the Windy Wing Pony.

Sweet Dreams, the So Soft Sleepy Newborn Pony.

**Soft Sleepy Newborn Ponies**
**Release year: Year Five (1986–87)**

Sure, some ponies are tiny, but some of them can be quite large as well. Meet the So Soft Sleepy Newborn Ponies, which were released in Year Five. You can see them as the pony counterpart of baby dolls except, well… they are ponies! They have the same eye mechanism as the Beddy Bye Eyes Ponies, which means that their eyes close when they are laid on their sides. In addition, their eyes also close when you brush their tails. They come with several accessories, such as a bonnet, pacifier and so on.

**Big Brother Ponies**
**Release year: Year Five to Seven (1986–89)**

Did you know that most G1 Ponies are actually female? In Year Five, however, we were introduced to the Big Brother Ponies, which are adult male ponies. They can be recognised by their bigger body and feathered hooves. The first two sets of Big Brother ponies were all themed after certain jobs, including Firefighter, Sailor, Policeman, and so on. They all came with a hat, bandana and comb. Three other adult ponies were released later as well under the Loving Family line as Daddy Ponies. There was also a mail order Big Brother Pony named Coat 'n Tails/Tux 'n Tails. Additionally, the UK got lucky with an exclusive Big Brother set. For more information about those, see the G1 Nirvana section on page 36.

Tex, a Year Five Big Brother Pony.

Barnacle, a Year Six Big Brother Pony. (Photograph by K. Bollmeier)

**Twice as Fancy Ponies**
**Release year: Year Five to Eight (1986–90)**

Ponies commonly have either a large symbol or a cluster of symbols on their hips. During Year Five (1986–87), however, Hasbro decided to mix up this concept with the addition of Twice as Fancy ponies (or TAF for short). These ponies have symbols that cover up most of their flanks, and some ponies even have symbols on their faces.

During the first two years that Twice as Fancy ponies were available, the assortment only covered regular-sized ponies, but Year Seven (1988–89) marked the introduction of Loving Family Ponies triple packs. The sets featured regular-sized Twice as Fancy Mummy and Daddy ponies, and debuted baby-sized TAF ponies. The babies had unique symbols that were a combination of the symbols from both their parents. Additionally, that same year a line of Europe-exclusive TAF babies was released that added additional brothers and sisters to the before mentioned babies.

In Year Eight (1989–90) the final wave of Twice as Fancy ponies was released, but only through mail order with Horseshoe points.[5] The line covered baby variants of the first set of six Twice as Fancy ponies from Year Five.

Sugarberry, a Twice-as-Fancy Pony, in packaging.

Twice-as-Fancy Munchy (left) and Night Glider (right).

**Sweetheart Sister Ponies**
**Release year: Year Seven to Ten (1988–92)**

In Year Seven we were introduced to the Sweetheart Sister Ponies. These ponies are a lot more slender than the regular ones, with the meaning behind this being that they are more like the teenagers of the *My Little Pony* world. Quite a number of Sweetheart Sister Ponies have been released, some under different set names as well, such as Pretty Ponies, Sweet Kisses Ponies and Sundazzle Ponies.

Sweet Sundrop, the Year Eight Prom Queen Sweetheart Sister Pony.

From left to right: Mayfair the Showtime Beauties Pony, Skyflier the Highflying Beauties Pony and Crystalline the Shimmering Beauties Pony. (Photograph by PirateParakeet)

**Dream Beauties**
**Release year: Year Eight (1989–90)**

Although looking completely different to normal ponies, the Dream Beauties are part of the official *My Little Pony* line-up as well. The idea with these is that they are grown-up My Little Ponies. Made of hard plastic instead of vinyl, they are taller than a normal *My Little Pony* figure and are much more horse-like. A total of eighteen Dream Beauties have been released in six different sets.

**Petite Ponies**
**Release year: Year Eight (1989–90)**

The Petite Ponies are small ponies made of hard plastic instead of soft vinyl, with most of them having sculpted manes instead of real hair, though some do have brushable tails. Their bodies have quite a lot of variation, with some of them having a pearlescent finish or translucent parts. They could be placed on special parts of playsets for Petite Ponies to activate several actions, like opening doors or rotating items.

Various types of Petite Ponies.

**Chuck E Cheese Pony**
**Release year: Year Eight (1989–90)**
**Set: Store Exclusive Ponies**

In the late 1980s people were able to exchange tickets from Chuck E Cheese restaurants for the exclusive Chuck E Cheese Baby Pony. This was the only way to get her as she wasn't available for retail. Her symbol is a white version of the Chuck E Cheese logo. This makes the pony very unique, as it's quite rare for a pony to get a symbol based on a company logo.

The pony has a logo of Chuck E Cheese as its symbol.

Pretty Puff, the Secret Surprise Pony.

**Secret Surprise Ponies**
**Release year: Year Nine (1990–91)**

Are ponies good at keeping secrets? One thing we know for sure is that the Secret Surprise Ponies certainly are. Released in Year Nine, these ponies are a bit larger than your regular pony. The secret of these ponies (no pun intended) is that they have a hidden compartment under their cape that can only be opened by using a key on their chest. In here you can store anything that fits, like perhaps a secret message on a piece of paper or a nice piece of jewellery. It can be quite hard to find a complete Secret Surprise Pony since the cape and key can get lost quite quickly.

**Teeny Tiny Baby Ponies**
**Release year: Year Nine and Ten (1990–92)**

You thought the baby ponies were small? Well, the ponies in Generation 1 can be even smaller, because in Year Nine Hasbro released the Teeny Tiny Baby Ponies. These ponies are the smallest G1 baby ponies ever released! Four single ponies were available in Year Nine and in Year Ten three sets of baby twins followed.

Rattles and Tattles, the Teeny Pony Twins.

Scale comparison with a normal and newborn baby pony.

**Rapunzel**
**Release year: Year Nine (1990–91)**
**Set: Mail Order Exclusive Ponies**

With the Horseshoe point program a lot of mail order exclusive ponies have been released, but one of them stands out the most – Rapunzel, who is considered the most valuable Generation 1 pony to be released in the United States. Like her name implies, she has long hair and her symbol resembles Rapunzel from the fairy tale looking out of the tower's window. She was available through the mail order program and you would receive one for just two Horseshoe points – and an additional $8.95. Nowadays she can go for incredibly high amounts, like $600 or higher!

*Above and right*: Rapunzel; note the symbol on her flank! (Photograph by Linda van Leeuwen)

**Baby Stockings**
**Release year: Year Nine (1990–91)**
**Set: Mail Order Exclusive Ponies**

Not all mail order exclusives were bought with Horseshoe points, though! In 1990 Hasbro partnered up with Kellogg's to distribute this white pony with bright red hair and a green stocking as her symbol in exchange for proof of purchase of Rice Krispies. The pony never got an official name but is most commonly known as Baby Stockings.

Baby Stockings, as she is commonly known. (Photograph by PirateParakeet)

From left to right: Fancy Mermaid Pony Baby Sea Shimmer, Baby Pearly and Baby Sea Princess. (Photograph by K. Bollmeier)

**Fancy Mermaid Ponies**
**Release year: Year Ten (1991–92)**

In Year Ten we were introduced to another kind of underwater ponies – the Fancy Mermaid Ponies. These were newborn ponies who were part pony and part mermaid, with their tails having a pearly finish. Three Mermaid Ponies have been released: Baby Pearly, Baby Sea Princess and Baby Sea Shimmer.

**Birthday Pony**
**Release year: Year Ten (1991–92)**

In Year Ten it was the 10th anniversary for the *My Little Pony* line. To celebrate Hasbro released the Birthday Pony. Her body is decorated with some festive decals and she also came with streamers in her hair. She even came with her own present, which included a locket, bracelet or hair clip, so it was always a surprise to see what gift she had for you!

The Birthday Pony, without streamers in her hair.

## Other Creatures and Characters

Besides ponies of all sizes, there are other creatures in the world of *My Little Pony*, most of which came bundled with playsets and other ponies. We found them too interesting not to talk about so below are some interesting *My Little Pony* creatures.

Did you know that a small crossover happened in the first generation? In Year Five the First-Tooth Baby Ponies were introduced, which came with accessories like a toothbrush and toothpaste, but one pony, named Baby North Star, came with a little glow-worm. For those who not know, *Glo Friends* was a toy line and television show that aired alongside the *My Little Pony and Friends* show during the 1980s. The *Glo Friends* brand was owned by Playskool/Hasbro, so while it wasn't a very exotic collaboration, it's still fun to see this kind of crossover.

Those who watch the G4 *Friendship is Magic* television series are perhaps familiar with Spike the Dragon, but the cute purple dragon actually made his first appearance in the first generation! He was released alongside Majesty and the Dream Castle playset in 1983. Another version of him was released as a mail order. But he wasn't the only dragon released during the first generation, as in Year Five the Princess Ponies released in the UK, Italy and several Scandinavian countries each came with a Dragon Friend.

While the international versions of the Princess Ponies came with dragons, what about the US versions? That brings us to a totally different kind of creature – the Bushwoolies. In 1985 we saw the first release of the *Escape from Katrina* television special, which introduced us to the Bushwoolies. They are fuzzy creatures who were held as slaves until Megan and the ponies saved them. In total six versions of them were made, but with only three unique moulds.

The glow-worm figure that came with Baby North Star.

G1 Spike (left) and G4 Spike (right).

Chumster (left) and Wishful (right) the Bushwoolies.

**Megan and Sundance**
**Release year: Year Three, Four and Seven (1984–86, 1988–89)**

Megan was a human who could travel to the world of the ponies and appeared often in the Generation 1 shows and movies. In the merchandise she was always released with Sundance, who was her special pony. Over the years several sets with Megan and Sundance have been released, which include:

- Year Three (1984–85): Regular Sundance and Megan.
- Year Four (1985–86): So Soft Sundance and Megan with a different dress and make up.
- Year Seven (1988–89): Twice as Fancy Sundance and Megan, who got a completely new look.

The Megan doll and Sundance.

**Molly and Baby Sundance**
**Release year: Year Four** (1985–86)

Megan wasn't the only human in the pony universe. In Year Four Molly was introduced, together with a Beddy Bye Eye Baby Sundance. Just like Megan, Baby Sundance was Molly's special pony. Being Megan's little sister, Molly is also smaller than her.

The Molly doll.

Baby Sundance has Beddy Bye Eyes. (Photograph by PirateParakeet)

**Pony Friends and Pretty Pals**
**Release year: Year Five to Seven (1986–89)**

*My Little Pony* is, of course, all about ponies, but did you know that other animal species existed too in G1? Starting in Year Five, two waves of Pony Friends introduced different animal species, including a lion, giraffe, llama and even a dinosaur. Visually, these animals were designed to fit the MLP style, with bright colours, symbols and adorable faces, but all with a unique mould.

In Year Seven the Pretty Pals replaced the Pony Friends name and bundled four new species each with a baby pony and some accessories. This final wave introduced a panda bear, sheep, calf and a kangaroo.

From left to right: Zig Zag the Zebra, Creamsicle the Giraffe and Kingsley the Lion.

Baby Nectar the Panda (left) and Baby Stripes (right).

## Nirvanas

Nirvanas are G1 ponies that have a very limited distribution and most of the time are exclusive to one certain country. This is because of two reasons: the first reason is that they were made exclusively for that country and the second is that they are actually produced in that country as well. For that second reason it might be wise to check the bottom of their hooves, since this tells you where the pony was produced and, as a result, if it's a Nirvana. Examples of countries that G1 Nirvanas were released in include Italy, Macau, France and Greece. The value of a Nirvana Pony really depends on where the pony comes from; for example, Italian ponies are a common find in Europe, and usually don't have a high value.

**Spanish Piggy Ponies**
**Release year: Year One and Two (1982–84)**

Spain is an example of a country who made their own ponies. They've made ponies with the same bodies as the regular ones, but they also made ponies with their own exclusive body. These are called Piggy Ponies due to the fact that their body has some similarities with that of a pig. In addition, they also have eyes that close when you put them on their side. They were made by Milton Bradley (MB) and Brekor.[6] People didn't know they were part of the *My Little Pony* line at first until one was spotted in packaging. There were Piggy Pony variations of several normal G1 ponies like Blossom and Minty, but some unique characters were also introduced like Perla and Fresita. Most of them also have variations, like different coloured hair or symbols.

Lemon Drop Piggy Pony.
(Photograph by Krystal Dulce)

Algodoncete Piggy Pony.
(Photograph by Krystal Dulce)

**Greek Ponies**
**Release year: Year Three (1984–85)**

In Greece the ponies were manufactured and sold by El Greco, who ran factories in Greece that would specifically make ponies under license for Hasbro for their country. Aside from Nirvana releases of internationally known ponies, El Greco also released several ponies that were exclusive to Greece.

Two of the Greek ponies are especially sought after: Ladybird and Candles (or Birthday). Both were released as part of the Greek Easter celebration, with the cultural background being recognised that the ladybird is the Greek symbol for Easter and spring, while candles are part of the Easter tradition.[7] They came in large red eggs, which is also part of the local tradition, and both ponies were moulded in the Bubbles/Seashell sitting post.

*Above*: Left to right: Greek Glory, Sunlight and Firefly. (Photograph by Linda van Leeuwen)

*Right*: Greek Lambaditsa/ Birthday Pony. (Photograph by Marina Strati)

Sara-Sara (left) and Pinky (right). (Photograph by Shelvesofwhimsy)

**Mai Ritoru Ponii – Osharena Ponii**
**Release year: 1985**

In the 1980s Hasbro and Japanese toy company Takara worked together and shared several licenses with each other. One of those licenses was the *My Little Pony* line and in 1985 Takara released the Mai Ritoru Ponii – Osharena Ponii series, which translates to 'My Little Pony – Styling Pony'. As you can see these ponies are totally different to your normal *My Little Pony*, with a more anthropomorphic look. These were in fact more like dolls that you could dress up in different outfits, which could be bought separately. Today these ponies are quite hard to find since they were only released in Japan. Several Fakies of these also exists, which are quite sought after by collectors.

**Mountain Boy Ponies**
**Release year: Year Six (1987–88)**

In 1987 Hasbro released the Mountain Boy Ponies, consisting of Fireball, Ice Crystal, Lightning, Sunburst, Thundercloud and Tornado. This set was exclusive to the United Kingdom, though it also appeared in Scandinavia. Their symbols are all themed after weather elements and they all have white freckles on the side of their faces. The fact that they were exclusively released in the UK makes them much harder to find and each can go for about $50+ online.

Mountain Boy Lightning (left), Thundercloud (top) and Tornado (right). (Photograph by K. Bollmeier)

**Surprise Twins Pony**
**Release year: Year Eleven (1993)**

The Surprise Twins Pony was released as a UK and Continental Europe exclusive pony. The unique concept of her is that she's pregnant with twins! When you press the button on her body her newborn twins will fall out. The twins are incredibly small and are actually worth a lot of money – even more sometimes than the mum! A playset was also made to match the Bed and Crib pony set.

Surprise Twins Pony, twins and the Bed and Crib Set. (Photograph by Linda van Leeuwen)

**Dutch Ponies**
**Release year: Year Thirteen (1995)**

We in the Netherlands actually had the honour of getting the final *My Little Pony* sets from the first generation! This line of ponies features eight regular-sized ponies and five baby-sized figures that only received Dutch and German names. There have been reports of sightings in Germany and Belgium, but the central distribution region was just the Netherlands.[8] Because of this small release they're commonly referred to as 'Dutch Ponies' and are pretty rare outside of Europe.

From left to right: Dutch Candy Pony/Snoepjes Pony, Love Pony and School Pony.

# Generation 2

The second generation of *My Little Pony* debuted in 1997. It was the first time that the *My Little Pony* line would receive a makeover with totally new bodies, which are a lot thinner than the previous moulds. Many collectors didn't like these changes since they were so different from the first generation. The second generation didn't sell that well in the United States, effectively staying on the shelves for only about two years. However, this generation was a lot more successful in Europe, where it lasted about six years. Because of this, many US collectors are especially interested in the ponies released after 1999 since they were only sold in Europe. One way to recognise a G2 pony is by looking at their eyes, as one of their key characteristics are their gem eyes. The value of the pony can drop significantly when they are missing.

Just like Generation 1, this generation is commonly categorised by release year in the collectors' community, counting 1997 as Year One.

From left to right: Light Heart, Hip Holly, Dash and Miss Painter.

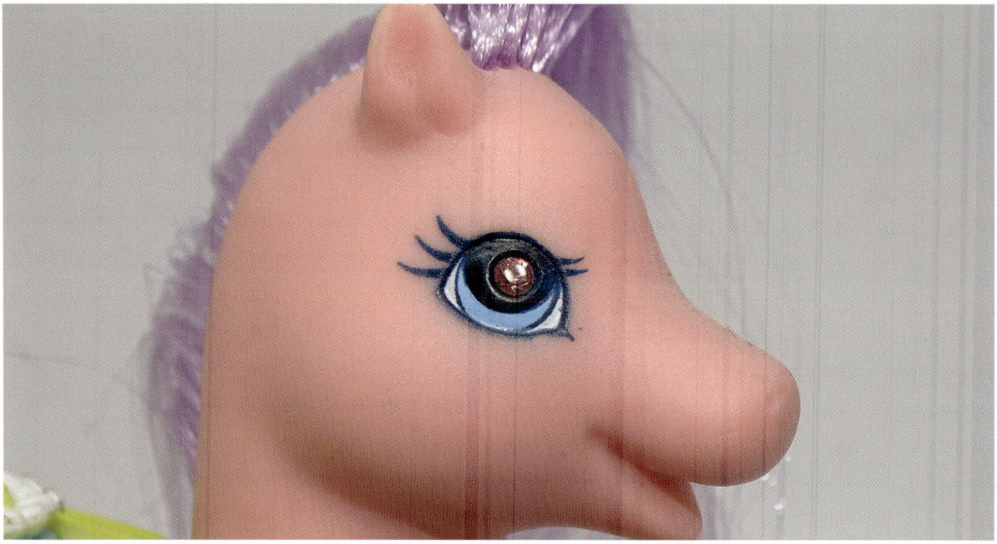

G2 Ponies can be quickly recognised by their jewel eyes.

## Highlights of Ponies and Sets

**Secret Surprise Friends**
**Release year: Year One (1997)**

Generation 2 saw the light of day in 1997, in the form of five ponies that are commonly referred to as Secret Surprise Friends. Berry Bright, Clever Clover, Morning Glory, Petal Blossom and Sky Shimmer each came with their own accessories. The ponies and extras were sold on a newly designed backcard too, featuring the new logo and more spacious blister packaging.

From left to right: Petal Blossom, Berry Bright and Morning Glory.

**Princess Silver Swirl and Baby Swirly**
**Release year: Year Four (2000)**
**Set: Light-Up Family**

Every *My Little Pony* set is unique, not only when it comes to colours, names and body types, but with features too. The Light-Up Family sets from 2000, which only appeared in Europe, featured four double packs of ponies and matching babies. The pony figures each have a unique light-up effect once you press on their symbols. One pony from this set is Princess Silver Swirl, who has a white body with silver coating, combined with tinsel-filled white hair and a light-up horn. All these factors make her a very unique pony that's beautiful to look at; though later, in Year Six (2002), Diamond Glow and Star Swirl shared her general design.

*Right*: Princess Silver Swirl from the Princess Ponies Series.

*Below*: Various releases of Princess Silver Swirl and Baby Swirly. (Photograph by Jessica M. Kriescher)

**Twin Baby Ponies**
**Release year: Year Four, Five and Seven (2000, 2001 and 2003)**

Most baby ponies released during the second generation of *My Little Pony* were part of the Twin Baby line. Each set contained twin ponies in baby size that have nearly matching body colours and symbol, but with variations in the pose or mane to keep them apart. An exception on this design can be found in the 2003 Play Area Twin Baby sets, which featured twin ponies with contrasting colours for their bodies and symbols. A final variation came with the sailing boat playset in 2003, in which the twin ponies share no similarities, aside from the symbol.

*Above*: Drifter and Dreamer the Twin Baby Ponies.

*Left*: Giggles and Wiggles the Royal Twin Baby Ponies.

**Unicorn Ponies with Magic Wings**
**Release year: Year Five and Six (2001–02)**

Although almost every G2 pony released after 1999 can be seen as 'valuable', one of the rarer lines is the Unicorn Ponies with Magic Wings. As seen on the photographs, this line consisted of unicorn ponies with clip-on wings. The ponies in the first release wave are Copper Glow, Silver Glow and Golden Glow, while the second set included Diamond Glow and a variant of Golden Glow. Copper Glow seems to be the most popular and sought after of them all, probably because her very unusual colour scheme.

The Year 5 Unicorn Ponies. From left to right: Copper Glow, Silver Glow and Golden Glow. (Photograph by Jessica M. Kriescher)

From left to right: Golden Glow (second version), Princess Twinkle Star and Princess Silver Swirl. (Photograph by Jessica M. Kriescher)

# Generation 3 and 3.5

## Generation 3

While the second generation wasn't that successful in the United States, Generation 3, which lasted from 2003 until 2009, has proven to be a far more successful change. The shape of the ponies changed again, but they resembled the body shapes of the Generation 1 ponies far more than those of the second generation. Generation 3 also introduced ponies with different sizes, such as Styling-Sized ponies. These ponies were about twice the size as normal ponies and came with much more hair, making it easier to style than on regular ponies. Smaller ponies were also introduced during G3 with the Ponyville line.

All My Heart, the 2007 Valentine's Day Pony.

Snowflake, the Target exclusive Winter Series Pony released in 2004. (Photograph by K. Bollmeier)

## Highlights of Ponies and Sets

**Holiday Ponies**
**Release year: 2003–09**

A common theme throughout Generation 3 of *My Little Pony* was the celebration of holidays. Every major release year had at least one holiday line, and from 2006 to 2008 there were even four holiday sets released during each year. The most common lines in the lifespan of the third generation were Easter and winter-themed sets, sometimes accompanied by Valentine's Day and Halloween ponies. The latter lines always contained two ponies each, whereas winter ranges had three yearly ponies. Easter varied from three to five per year, making those ponies the most common to find.

Winter Minty from 2008 was one of the more popular G3 ponies.

The 2006 Spring Basket containing (from left to right) Berries n' Cherries, Spring Carnivale and Lavender Cloud. (Photograph by K. Bollmeier)

**Jewel Ponies**
**Release year: 2004–07**

The Jewel Ponies are, as you might have guessed, recognisable by their jewel. This large jewel is the centrepiece of the pony's cutie mark, and each pony has a different colour and cutie mark combination. In total thirty Jewel Ponies have been released in the few years they were produced, including a Toys "R" Us exclusive birthday set featuring a Jewel Pony for every month of the year. Additionally, one Jewel Pony, Sunshimmer, was only available through mail order when trading in sixteen points from other *My Little Pony* products, much like the G1 Horseshoe point program.

Wondermint (left) and the mail order exclusive Sunshimmer (right), both of which are Jewel Ponies.

Azalia Bloom the Breezie (left) and Sunset Breezie, a G4 Breezie (right).

**Breezies**
**Release year: 2006–07**

A new subspecies was also launched during the third generation, called Breezies. Just like the G1 Flutter and Winger Ponies they were much smaller than normal ponies, being about the size of a small bird. They have several bug-like elements, such as antennas and fabric wings, combined with a pony body. They were occasionally packed with a normal pony, but some of them were also released with other Breezies. The creatures eventually made a comeback in Generation 4 with a much more slender design and translucent plastic wings.

**Ponyville Ponies**
**Release year: 2006–10**

A radically different spin-off of *My Little Pony* figures was launched in 2006 called Ponyville. Smaller ponies that were fully moulded in plastic opened the door to detailed, cheaper and smaller playsets, while still carrying the *My Little Pony* charm. While many people disliked the big difference with regular pony figures, others liked the smaller scale or world-building aspect of it.

Later on, ponies were released with removable/interchangeable manes, as well as ponies in anthropomorphic poses. In 2010 two sets of blind bags were launched as part of Ponyville, which shortly after evolved into the huge (twenty-four sets) line of blind bag figures in the fourth generation.

Various Ponyville figures, including mermaid Scootaloo and an anthropomorphic Sweetie Belle.

**25th Anniversary Collector Set**
**Release year: 2008**

When counting 1983 as the official start, 2008 marked the 25th birthday for the *My Little Pony* line. To celebrate Hasbro released several G3 singles as well as a large Collectors Set containing the Core 7 Ponies of G3. Each pony was decorated with an inspirational word alongside some other decals like swirls or hearts.

The 25th Birthday Celebration Collector Set, MIB.

The Black and Blue Art Pony. (Photograph by K. Bollmeier)

**The First or Black and Blue Art Pony**
**Release year: 2008**
**Set: Art Ponies**

In 2008 Hasbro released their first Art Pony. These ponies were aimed towards collectors, with their unusual and often detailed decals. The first one doesn't have a specific name and is just often referred to as the 'First' Art Pony or the 'Black and Blue' one. Its hair is blue, and its body and eyes are completely black, but are covered with blue decals. The box is decorated the same way to make a matching combination.

**Pop Art Pony**
**Release Year: 2008**
**Set: Art Ponies**

This Art Pony was based on the popular pop art period. As shown, its colours are vibrant, with a high contrast between blue and orange, and it is decorated with several stars and lightning decals. Just like the other Art Ponies this one too has a matching box. It was available for order on HasbroToyShop.com for $12.99.

The pop art-inspired Art Pony is quite the statement piece!

The underwater-inspired Art Pony is incredibly elegant, featuring marine life on her sides.

**Underwater Pony**
**Release Year: 2008**
**Set: Art Ponies**

Where the Pop Art Pony was very clashing and abstract when it came to the colours and shapes, the Underwater Pony was more organic in terms of decals and its colour palette. As the name suggests, this pony has an underwater theme, with her hair and body colours matching that of the underwater world. The sides and part of the head are decorated with a highly detailed underwater scene featuring several fish and underwater plants. Just like the Pop Art Pony, this one was also available for order on HasbroToyShop.com.

**Junko Mizuno Collector Pony**
**Release year: 2009**
**Set: Collectors' Ponies**

This pony was designed by famous manga artist Junko Mizuno during the My Little Pony Project: 25 Ponies for 25 Years. Comparable to the Pony Project in 2005, famous artists were able to design their own 18-inch pony and these one-of-a-kind pieces were then auctioned off for the Give Kids the World Village charity. The Junko Mizuno Pony was eventually released in the usual *My Little Pony* scale as part of the collector line. Along with the unique decals on her body, she also wears high heels and a fur bonnet.

Manga artist Junko Mizuno created this pony, inspired by her gothic kawaii style.

The original blank pony that artists could decorate for the event. (Photograph by Stephanie McPhie)

**Ribbons and Hearts Pony (aka Breast Cancer Awareness Pony)**
**Release year: 2010**
**Set: Never released**

This pony is quite a mystery. It was released on eBay together with several other ponies who turned out to be the 2010 convention and fair exclusives. It's most likely that these had been taken straight from the factory. At one point Hasbro was asked about the pony but there were not yet plans to release her at that point, though they had the idea to work together with a charity and release them that way. Due the fact that it's now eight years later and we're far into the fourth generation, it's very unlikely that she will ever be released in the future.

While never released, two variants of the pony were spotted – one with an open mouth and the other closed. Her eyes have a pink ribbon decal on them and her cutie mark is a real ribbon with a heart on top of it. The closed variants have also been spotted in packaging which calls her the Ribbons and Hearts Pony.[9]

Two versions of Ribbons and Hearts, one with the mouth open and one with it closed. (Photograph by Stephanie McPhie)

## Exclusive Ponies

**Pony Project Ponies**
**Release year: 2005**
**Set: Convention and Fair Exclusives**

In 2005 a *My Little Pony*-themed art project took place in Milk Gallery in New York, where artists displayed their unique take on decorating a blank *My Little Pony* figure. As part of this event Hasbro released three exclusive ponies in New York.

The base design for all three is a figure without any detailing, a red mane, a heart instead of an eye and no cutie mark. Instead the ponies have 'The Pony Project' and a little heart printed on their flanks. Both a white and a black variant were made, and a Twice as Fancy design too. The latter did not feature a specific cutie mark, but instead had several everyday symbols like a hamburger, dollar sign and pencil. Each pony came with a brush matching the pony's body colour.

At the San Diego Comic Con that year the white pony project figure was again available to the public in a limited stock of just 2,000 pieces.[10]

The black base design for the Pony Project. (Photograph by Caitlin Beam)

**Comic Con 2007 Pony**
**Release year: 2007**
**Set: Convention and Fair Exclusives**

After a year of absence, Hasbro returned with another San Diego Comic Con exclusive in 2007. This masked hero pony has a red body but wears a blue mask and a yellow and orange suit with blue accents that covers up her entire body, except for the face. Her cutie mark is the G3 *My Little Pony* logo with 'Power' added and she has a red and yellow mane.

The 'Power' pony produced for SDCC 2007. (Photograph by K. Bollmeier)

The ninja-inspired pony, featuring her comic book-style decoration.

**Comic Con 2008 Pony**
**Release year: 2008**
**Set: Convention and Fair Exclusives**

Another comic-styled pony this year as the annual SDCC exclusive, this time in ninja style with a pink mane, black body and pink mask. She does not feature an actual cutie mark, but has a two-sided 'comic' of both her regular self and the masked version on her flanks. Both designs are also featured on the box she came in, which sadly has no window to peek at the pony while keeping the seal intact.

**Comic Con 2009 Pony**
**Release year: 2009**
**Set: Convention and Fair Exclusives**

This pony was released for the 2009 San Diego Comic Con and was also for sale online after the convention at HasbroToyShop.com. This pony was quite unique as it has two different sides – one superhero themed and the other villain themed. The superhero part comprises a yellow pony with a pink and green outfit, while on the flank there's a speech balloon that says, 'I'll save the day!' The villain side is all purple with flames, and the speech balloon on this side proclaims, 'I'll rule the world!' The packaging was also split into two sides; however, the sides where actually swapped so when you look at the superhero side of the pony, you'll see the villain design of the box, and vice versa.

*Right and overleaf above*: The split superhero/villain pony released for SDCC 2009.

**Comic Con 2010 Pony**
**Release year: 2010**
**Set: Convention and Fair Exclusives**

During the San Diego Comic Con of 2010 Hasbro presented early art and designs of Generation 4, but since the first episode had not aired yet, the SDCC exclusive for that year was based on the G3 mould. The pink-haired pony has a white body that's used as a canvas for graffiti-style decals, covering her flank, legs and face. A rare concept variant of this pony was found online prior to the release at SDCC that year, featuring the same body as the final version but a cyan mane and tail instead of pink. Aside from some prototypes, this version was never released.

The 'graffiti' pony. (Photograph by Caitlin Beam)

This pony is often referred to as the Gothic Tattoo Pony – you can see why!

**Comic Con 2011 Pony**
**Release year: 2011**
**Set: Convention and Fair Exclusives**

This pony was released for the 2011 San Diego Comic Con and was also for sale online after the convention at HasbroToyShop.com. Her body is translucent with a black gradient. Lots of decals are also present all over the body. Because of this she's sometimes referred to as the 'Gothic Tattoo Pony'. What's quite interesting is that this pony was of the Generation 3 mould, despite Generation 4 already blooming, resulting in a G4 *My Little Pony* logo on the box.

***My Little Pony* Fair 2005 Pony**
**Release year: 2005**
**Set: Convention and Fair Exclusives**

In 2005 the first exclusive pony for the *My Little Pony* fair was produced. Bay Breeze was exclusive to the visitors at that year's fair, resulting in a production run of only 300 pieces. She has a 3D flower cutie mark and the pony is scented too.

Bay Breeze, with her 3D flower cutie mark. (Photograph by Caitlin Beam)

**_My Little Pony_ Fair 2006 Ponies**
**Release year: 2006**
**Set: Convention and Fair Exclusives**

At the 2006 *My Little Pony* fair two exclusive ponies were revealed, both paying a homage to the location of that year's fair – San Francisco! Both ponies are a custom variant of Love Wishes, who Hasbro originally handed out for the fair. The difference between the two is in the cutie mark: Frisco has an icon of the Golden Gate Bridge and Trolley has one of the cable car.

Originally 150 Frisco characters were made for the fair, but due to huge popularity they sold out quickly. In addition, 100 Trolley ponies were sold, which was raised to 150 after the fair. The extra ponies were named Trolley 2.0 to not conflict with the original set of 100.[11]

Frisco (left) and Trolley (right). (Photograph by Caitlin Beam)

Love Wishes, the mail order pony Frisco and Trolley were based on.

**_My Little Pony_ Fair 2007 Pony (Pinkie Pie)**
**Release year: 2007**
**Set: Convention and Fair Exclusives**

The special pony for the 2007 *My Little Pony* Fair, which was held in Memphis, Tennessee, and at Ponycon in Bristol, UK, was a familiar pony; familiar, yet exclusive, as this Pinkie Pie pony features a special decorative cutie mark on one side and leaves on the other side in similar colours. Her body is pink, but with white gradients around her legs, tail and ears. Both her face and hind legs have some additional decals too, and her mane and tail have tinsel mixed in.

The white-gradient Pinkie Pie with additional decals. (Photograph by Caitlin Beam)

*Above left*: Providence, the US version. (Photograph by K. Bollmeier)

*Above right*: Sunny Grace, the UK version. (Photograph by Caitlin Beam)

**_My Little Pony_ Fair 2008 Ponies**
**Release year: 2008**
**Set: Convention and Fair Exclusives**

For the *My Little Pony* Fair in 2008, two different ponies were created, one being exclusive for the US Pony Fair, and the other for the one in the United Kingdom. Both followed the same design, being completely decorated with swirls, flowers and heart symbols, but in different colours. The US pony had a more monotone look, with different shades of pink, while the UK variant had much more contrast by having a white body and decals all in black, with its hair in yellow.

**_My Little Pony_ Fair 2009 Pony (aka Peacock Pony)**
**Release year: 2009**
**Set: Convention and Fair Exclusives**

In 2009 fans of *My Little Pony* could go to Las Vegas, Nevada, or Sheffield, UK, to get their very own Peacock Pony. A bright green mane combined with a white body and metallic blue hind legs form the canvas on which a beautiful peacock cutie mark is placed, covering her legs and body. The blue and green colour scheme is also found in her tail and eyeshadow.

Peacock Pony was the first *My Little Pony* Fair pony that featured a see-through display box, which made it possible to display the pony from within the packaging without breaking the seal. Earlier ponies were sold in plastic bags and generic cardboard boxes.

Peacock Pony; elegant but striking. (Photograph by K. Bollmeier)

**_My Little Pony_ Fair 2010 Pony (aka Dandelion Pony)**
**Release year: 2010**
**Set: Convention and Fair Exclusives**

A brightly coloured pony, commonly referred to as Dandelion, was available at the 2010 *My Little Pony* Fair. While this was at the edge between G3 and G4, this pony is fully styled as a Generation 3 pony. Its body is a gradient between two shades of green and has lots of floral decals and pink butterflies.

Dandelion, featuring numerous decals on her two-tone green body. (Photograph by K. Bollmeier)

**_My Little Pony_ Fair 2011 Pony (aka Egyptian Pony)**
**Release year: 2011**
**Set: Convention and Fair Exclusives**

This pony was released as an exclusive for the 2011 *My Little Pony* Fair, which was hosted at Hasbro's headquarters in Pawtucket, Rhode Island. She's often named the Egyptian Pony due her designs and colours. On her back is written 'MLP Fair 2011'.

The Egyptian Pony, both in and out of the box.

## Generation 3.5

Generation 3.5 is often referred to as one of the lesser, if not least favourite of the generations among fans. Where G3 had a lot of various characters, G3.5 focused only on the ponies from the show, which are often called the Core 7. These ponies include Pinkie Pie, Cheerilee, Rainbow Dash, Toola Roola, Scootaloo, Sweetie Belle and Starshine. Instead of different characters, Generation 3.5 was more about gimmicks as the ponies would be the same most of the time, except with a different gimmick and/or design like moulded interchangeable hair and different decals printed on the body.

Alongside normal ponies, Baby Ponies were also released in scale with the normal brushables.

*Right*: Starsong, a single figure that came with an activity book.

*Below*: Newborn Cutie Ponies also appeared in Generation 3.5: Pinkie Pie (left) and Starsong (right).

Pinkie Pie Twice-as-Fancy Pony.

**Twice as Fancy Ponies**
**Release year: 2009**

One line of Generation 3.5 featured ponies with large cutie marks on their flanks, other symbols and their name in a decorative style. While Hasbro did not give the line a specific name, collectors tend to name them Twice as Fancy, after the G1 ponies with a similar style. The complete Core 7 was released, each with their own unique flank design.

**Mother Ponies**
**Release year: 2009 and 2010**

Whereas basically all figures in G3.5 are part of the Core 7, there was a small exception to this rule. In 2009 and 2010 three sets were released that introduced the mothers of Rainbow Dash, Pinkie Pie and that of Cheerilee and Scootaloo. The mothers were combined with their children in baby form and all sets came with rolling accessories: Rainbow Dash's mother can push a shopping cart, a convertible car is included with Pinkie Pie's set and the mother of Cheerilee and Scootaloo has a stroller.

From left to right: mothers of Rainbow Dash, Pinkie Pie and Cheerilee/Scootaloo. (Photograph by K. Bollmeier)

# Generation 4

Generation 4 was introduced alongside a new television series called *My Little Pony: Friendship is Magic*. The series focuses on a pony called Twilight Sparkle who gets sent to Ponyville to learn about the Magic of Friendship. Together with her friends Applejack, Fluttershy, Pinkie Pie, Rarity and Rainbow Dash, she uses the power of friendship to help other ponies and to defeat evil. The combined bunch of ponies is commonly referred to as the 'Mane Six'. During this generation a new kind of fan started to appear – Bronies, a group of primarily male fans older than the core demographic of the *Friendship is Magic* series. In the later years of Generation 4 especially, it's clear that Hasbro noticed that *My Little Pony* has gotten a much more varied target demographic, reaching from infants to adults, regardless of gender. The series eventually became so popular that in 2017 *My Little Pony: The Movie* was released in cinemas all around the world.

The Mane Six from left to right: Applejack, Fluttershy, Pinkie Pie, Rainbow Dash, Rarity and Twilight Sparkle.

## Highlights of Ponies and Sets

**Friendship is Magic Gift Set**
**Release year: 2010**

In 2010, around the beginning of the *My Little Pony: Friendship is Magic* television show, the very first set in the fourth generation was this Friendship is Magic Gift Set. You might expect the first release to be an example of what the new generation was going to be, but as you can see this was quite something else. All of the figures included in the set have a moulded mane, which is something that only reappeared a handful of times later in the series. The characters included are Applejack, Pinkie Pie, Twilight Sparkle, Spike and a pink variant of Princess Celestia. This leaves Fluttershy, Rarity and Rainbow Dash out, who got their introduction release a bit later in the form of single figures. Also included was a small storybook, which shows a Friendship is Magic logo that differs from the one used in the show and on merchandise.

The Friendship is Magic Gift Set. It is interesting to note that not all of the Mane Six were included in this set – though Rainbow Dash features on the cover of the storybook if you look closely! (Photograph by Victor A. Ramirez)

Fashion Style Applejack with her accessories. (Photograph by Satu)

**Fashion Style Applejack**
**Release year: 2010**
**Set: Original Series Fashion Styles**

Together with the debut of *My Little Pony: Friendship is Magic*, the first figures of the show characters started to appear in stores, one of which was the Fashion Style Applejack figure seen here. As the popularity of the show started to climb, Hasbro continued to release new characters, and different variants of earlier released ponies too. Only later collectors noticed that this Applejack stood out from almost every figure that was released after her: she has a hat. Even though the hat's colour is not even remotely like her brown leather hat from the television show, it made this figure quite different from later releases. This uniqueness combined with the small production run makes the figure popular within the collectors' community.

**Early Non-Mane Six Ponies**
**Release year: 2011**
**Set: Original Series Singles and Original Series Bonus Sets**

At the start of the new generation, the new main characters, the Mane Six, got the most attention so as to introduce people to the new television series. In 2011 we saw a shift in characters as Hasbro rapidly started to release new characters, primarily in the line of assorted single ponies. Most of the ponies released during this period later on turned out to be rather exclusive as Hasbro did not release new figures of the characters. Except for Cheerilee, most ponies did not even get a proper appearance in the show, making the figures even more collectible. Ponies like Honeybuzz, Twinkleshine and Blossomforth are still very much wanted for this reason.

From left to right: Honeybuzz, Minty, Glimmer Wings Ploomette, Star Swirl and Lulu Luck.

Other new ponies from the early waves of G4 came bundled with existing Mane Six ponies in the form of bonus packs, and in this way ponies like Rainbow Flash, Skywishes and Star Swirl were introduced. Most of the ponies were not only exclusive for the bonus sets, but they were only available outside of the United States too.

**Toys "R" Us Collector Series**
**Release year: 2012-2013**

*My Little Pony* has known many short series of store-exclusive figures, and one of the more popular lines was the Collector Series that was available at Toys "R" Us stores worldwide during 2012 and 2013. The sets were easily recognisable by the alternate box designs, which featured bright pink borders. Two large multipacks were included in this exclusive series, featuring popular villains Nightmare Moon and Queen Chrysalis and other fan-favourite ponies from the *My Little Pony: Friendship is Magic* television show.

Along with these packs, two special regular-sized single figure were also released as part of this line. In 2012 the first, and so far only, Zecora brushable was released, with a glow-in-the-dark body and correct markings and jewellery to match her animated counterpart. Later, in 2013, a single Rainbow Dash figure was released at Toys "R" Us with the Shadowbolt costume, as seen in the show.

Finally, the exclusive line included two talking princess ponies, the first being a colour-correct re-release of Princess Celestia, and the second being the first talking Nightmare Moon. For unknown reasons Princess Celestia did not feature a matching box to go with the Collector Series line, even though she was a Toys "R" Us exclusive at the time.

*Above*: The second Collector Series set to be released containing Queen Chrysalis, Princess Cadance, Shining Armor, Lyrica, Lyra, Diamond Tiara and Derpy/Muffins. (Set provided by Celestiafan)

*Right*: The Collector Series Glow-in-the-Dark Zecora.

The Collector Series Talking Nightmare Moon. (Pony provided by Celestiafan)

**Rare Rainbow Power Ponies**
**Release year: 2014**
**Set: Rainbow Power Singles and Fashion Styles**

A new Applejack Fashion Style was released in 2014, together with the first Daisy Dreams Fashion Style pony. The new release introduced a correctly coloured hat, but both figures were barely available in stores, most of which were only spotted outside of the United States. All this resulted in another large demand for the Applejack figure – and to a lesser degree Daisy Dreams too – on online marketplaces.

The same situation also influenced the popularity and demand for the Neon Holly Dash and Rarity single ponies that were released around the same time. These too were mainly found outside the US, and to make things worse: this was Holly Dash's debut in the G4 toy line. Even today the prices of these ponies are significantly higher than comparable brushables.

Holly Dash Rainbow Power single. (Pony provided by Celestiafan)

Applejack Rainbow Power Fashion Style.

**Nurse Redheart**
**Release year: 2014, 2015 and 2016**
**Set: Walgreens Exclusive Singles**

A regular Nurse Redheart brushable was spotted for the first time on the online Chinese marketplace Taobao in June 2014. It was revealed during the San Diego Comic Con not long after that she would become available as a Walgreens exclusive pony.

For three years straight since then, a new Nurse Redheart was officially revealed during the SDCC. A common theme was that each release of her would be made in the same gimmick as the other ponies of that year's line. The following versions have been released:

- Rainbow Rocks (2014): A regular Nurse Redheart brushable.
- Cutie Mark Magic (2015): Includes a ribbon in her hair covered with her Cutie Mark.
- Explore Equestria (2016): A translucent body with a pearly coating and glitter.

Rainbow Power, Explore Equestria and Cutie Mark Magic releases of Nurse Redheart. (Photograph by Victor A. Ramirez)

**Guardians of Harmony/Fan Series**
**Release year: 2016 onward**

With the introduction of Generation 4, it was clear that more adult collectors were interested in the *My Little Pony* line, and especially the *Friendship is Magic* television series. While there were already plenty of brushable figures of several popular characters, fans of the show often criticized them for not being show-accurate due to their brushable hair and being too much oriented towards children. As a response Hasbro released the Guardians of Harmony line in 2016. With this line Hasbro wanted to create more gender-neutral toys that could be enjoyed by everyone. The regular Guardians of Harmony line consists of more action figure-like toys with sculpted manes and several points of articulation and gimmicks.

Aside from the regular line Hasbro also released a sub-line called the Guardians of Harmony Fan Series, which was eventually changed to just Fan Series later. The Fan Series line consist of high-quality sculptures of popular characters and moments from the show in dynamic poses. These figures contain barely any articulation and are meant for display only. The characters released so far are:

- Princess Celestia
- Nightmare Moon
- Discord and his throne
- Queen Chrysalis and several Changelings
- DJ Pon-3 with a turntable
- The Storm King and Grubber
- Tempest Shadow and Twilight Sparkle
- Trixie and Starlight Glimmer on a rocket

Princess Celestia Fan Series figure. (Photograph by Victor A. Ramirez)

Queen Chrysalis and the Changelings Fan Series figure.

Twilight Sparkle Versus Tempest Shadow Fan Series figure. (Photograph by Victor A. Ramirez)

A sealed MIB Fashion Style Muffins can fetch quite a price!

## Exclusive Ponies

**Fashion Style Muffins (also known as Derpy)**
**Release year: 2012**
**Set: San Diego Comic Con Exclusives**

Ever since the first episode of *My Little Pony: Friendship is Magic*, Muffins has been a fan favourite character that had recurring appearances in the show. Despite her popularity, very few figures of her have been released over the years. The first figure, this 6-inch-tall 'Fashion Style', was released at the 2012 San Diego Comic Con. It shouldn't come as a surprise that the combination of a popular character, a first release and low stock means that this figure was highly sought after. Over time more collectors started to sell the figure, but a sealed MIB Muffins still has quite some value.

**Swarovski DJ Pon-3**
**Release year: 2013**
**Set: San Diego Comic Con Exclusives**

Glitter accents and decorations are pretty common to see in the world of *My Little Pony* figures, especially when looking at the high amount of blind bag figures that have been released since the start of the fourth generation. When looking at annual exclusive figures, glitter must have been too common a decoration in Hasbro's eyes. The solution? Taking it to the next level with a 6-inch-tall DJ Pon-3 figure that's been decorated with original Swarovski crystals and lots of glitter. The combination of white and blue with the crystals gives this figure a very shiny and luxurious look. The box is designed as a discotheque, which fits the character of DJ Pon-3 perfectly, and is fitted with a light-up base underneath.

DJ Pon-3 looks incredible in this disco-inspired box. She has Swarovski crystals in her horn and glasses. (Pony provided by Celestiafan)

**Swarovski Princess Twilight Sparkle**
**Release year: 2013**
**Set: Special Releases**

In the same year that Hasbro released the SDCC Exclusive DJ Pon-3 figure, another interesting release appeared in Hasbro's own web store. This 6-inch release of Twilight Sparkle is referred to as an 'Adult Collectible', mainly because this figure features embedded Swarovski crystals as well. The stones richly decorate her wings, and her forehead, crown, necklace, cutie mark and hoofs are dipped in glitter to give her an even shinier look.

As can be seen, the box design features a level underneath the pony, much like the DJ Pon-3 box, but this one has no light-up effect.

*Above and below*: Twilight Sparkle with Swarovski crystals in her wings, both in and out of the box. (Pony provided by Celestiafan)

**Mane-Iac Mayhem Exclusives**
**Release year: 2014**
**Set: San Diego Comic Con Exclusives**

2014 was the year fans of the *My Little Pony: Friendship is Magic* series were introduced to Power Ponies, the superhero personas of the Mane Six. Mane-Iac Mayhem was introduced in the story arc as the main villain, who uses her special mane powers, hair gadgets and hair-inspired henchmen to steal an orb from the Maretropolis Museum. This unique story and appearance turned her into a very popular character after the episode aired, and she got the honour of getting two exclusive releases at SDCC that year.

The first figure is a two-pack with Spike the Dragon dressed as his comic book alter ego Humdrum. Mane-Iac is fitted with large moulded hair that closely resembles her hairstyle from the TV show and her costume is accentuated with a glitter coating. The accompanying Spike is glitter decorated too and comes with a small removable cape.

Mane-Iac Mayhem got an exclusive Equestria Girls release too, which is odd considering that she never appeared in any of the movies. Even with the lack of a developed Equestria Girls character, the doll turned out great. With large strands of hair, an equally large dress and gold-accented clothing, this is an impressive doll to see. Do note that the wild strands of hair are loose and inside the box they're fastened to the cardboard. If you're planning on displaying her in-character, it's best to keep her in the packaging.

Speaking of which, as with the other SDCC exclusive releases these figures come in unique boxes unlike any others. Both show a partially open design with a large Mane-Iac Mayhem face on the front and specially designed *My Little Pony* logos to go with the green colour scheme of Mane-Iac.

The Mane-Iac Mayhem and Spike as Humdrum set. (Photograph by Victor A. Ramirez)

The Mane-Iac Equestria Girls doll. (Photograph by Victor A. Ramirez)

**Chinese New Year Pinkie Pie**
**Release year: 2014**
**Set: Special Releases**

To celebrate the Chinese New Year in 2014, Hasbro released this Toys "R" Us exclusive Chinese Pinkie Pie due to the fact that 2014 was the year of the horse. This Pinkie Pie stands 8 inches tall and wears a red outfit decorated with Chinese designs. Along with a green comb, she came in a large box that matches her Chinese design.

The Chinese Pinkie Pie variant released for Chinese New Year – the year of the horse in 2014!

Chicken Pinkie Pie. (Photograph by Victor A. Ramirez)

**Nightmare Night Pinkie Pie**
**Release year: 2015**
**Set: San Diego Comic Con Exclusives**

As you can read on the previous pages, every year the SDCC exclusive announcements are always an exciting moment to look forward to. In 2015 Hasbro decided to give out various teasers towards this moment, and after some tense days the announcement was out: the SDCC 2015 exclusive was going to be a 6-inch chicken-costumed Pinkie Pie that comes in a bucket – and no, this year was not sponsored by a fast food chain. The Pinkie Pie figure wears the costume that she wore in the television show during Nightmare Night, the *My Little Pony* equivalent of Halloween, complete with a beak, feather suit and chicken legs, and she even comes with a candy bag.

**Equestria Girls Sci-Twi**
**Release year: 2015**
**Set: San Diego Comic Con Exclusives**

The second Comic Con Equestria Girl doll was the Sci-Twi doll, which stands for Science Twilight Sparkle. Within the Equestria Girls universe, this version of Twilight Sparkle was the one who lived in the human world. This set came with a locker and her faithful companion Spike the Dog, who is covered in glitter.

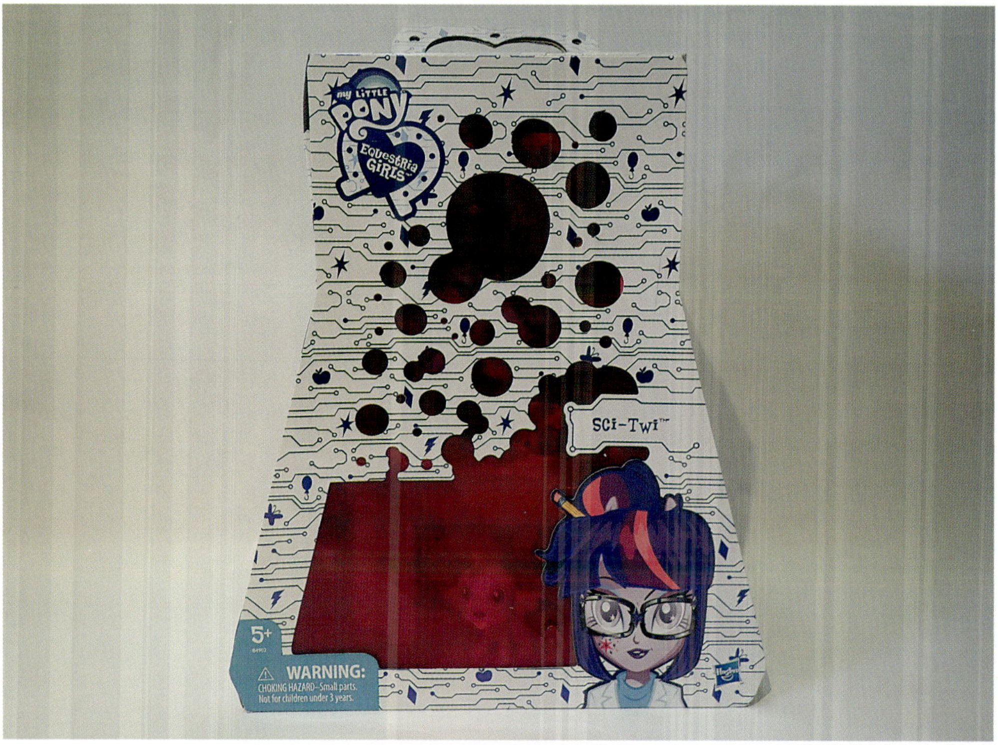

*Above and left*: Equestria Girls 'Sci-Twi', with Spike the Dog. (Photograph by Victor A. Ramirez)

The Guardians of Harmony Discord figure, bundled with Fluttershy and MIB.

**Guardians of Harmony Discord and Fluttershy**
**Release year: 2016**
**Set: San Diego Comic Con Exclusives**

The aforementioned Guardians of Harmony Discord figure was re-released later that year as the annual SDCC exclusive figure, and while a re-release as an exclusive sounds odd, Hasbro pulled it off to make this figure something special.

The first feature of this SDCC release is the large box that it comes in, fitted with a style that's unique to the fourth generation of *My Little Pony* figures. The box isn't just for packaging, as it contains a light-up base too, which is ideal to accentuate the detailed figures; most figures that have been sold are still in their original packaging due to this fact.

Discord itself is repainted when compared to the first release and is still seen in his iconic pose, holding a glass of chocolate milk. He is bundled with the only regular Guardians of Harmony Fluttershy figure released to date.

## Reboot Series

At the end of 2016, a new kind of ponies was spotted on an Asian online marketplace. No one at the time knew what was going on; some believed they were fake, others believed they were Happy Meal toys. But by taking a closer look we discovered that they had Hasbro's official production code under their hooves. For us it was clear that Hasbro was about to change the look of the Generation 4 ponies. The designs of the new ponies were more slender, and some of them had open mouths as well. Since no official set name was given they have been given the name 'Reboot Series' ponies. All ponies from 2017 onward used the new mould, with the exception of some old re-releases.

From left to right: Reboot Series Soarin', Applejack and Princess Celestia.

## *My Little Pony: The Movie*

The fourth generation of *My Little Pony* became extremely popular among children and collectors all over the world and this eventually led to the release of *My Little Pony: The Movie* in 2017. The film is about the Mane Six, who have to travel to foreign lands to get help with defeating Tempest Shadow and the Storm King. The film also introduced the return of a special kind of G1 ponies – the Seaponies. However, their appearance actually matches those of the Mermaid Ponies, and because of this some collectors like to refer them as 'Merponies' instead. With a new film out, a lot of merchandise was also being released, with most of them themed towards the Seaponies. There was also some merchandise related to Songbird Serenade, a character that was inspired and voiced by singer-songwriter Sia.

From left to right: Tempest Shadow, Sea Poppy, Seapony Princess Skystar and Seapony Rarity.

Ilona's Seapony display, which shows some of the released Seaponies.

**Haven Bay**
**Release year: 2017**
**Set: Walmart Exclusive Canterlot and Seaquestria Castle Playset**

One of the first toys released for the 2017 film was the Canterlot and Seaquestria playset, a very large playset that combined the two kingdoms together – that of the normal ponies and that of the Seaponies. The set officially came with Queen Novo and Spike the Pufferfish. A few months after its release a new variant suddenly popped up on Walmart's website. This exclusive variant came with lots of new accessories and three additional ponies: Princess Celestia, Twilight Sparkle and Haven Bay. Haven Bay was a completely new character that hadn't been released before, most likely as she did not have a large role in the movie. But a new pony is a new pony and several people were disappointed as they had already gotten the original playset without the bonus figures. The playset itself was expensive during its release, with a price tag of $88 (US), so those who wanted Haven Bay had to buy the whole playset again or buy her loose from sites like eBay – but she wasn't cheap there either.

The Haven Bay Seapony figure.

The Amazon exclusive Glitter Seapony Pinkie Pie figure.

**Glitter Seapony Pinkie Pie**
**Release year: 2017**
**Set: *My Little Pony: The Movie***

To celebrate the release of the 2017 *My Little Pony* film, Hasbro released this Glitter Seapony Pinkie Pie as an Amazon exclusive. This Pinkie Pie is on the same scale as the regular Glitter and Style Seaponies, but this exclusive version comes completely covered in glitter, as does as her pet, Gummy. Her tail is also made out of real fabric and her packaging includes a white base that lights up when you press the button.

## Blind Bags and the Friendship is Magic Collection

Since Generation 3, mini ponies have been a thing, so it was more than likely that the trend would continue with the fourth generation. The blind bags have proven that. The term 'blind bags' comes from the fact that they were released in surprise bags first; you had no idea which pony you would get, hence the term. However, there was a trick to find out which pony each bag contains. Every bag has a certain code printed on it, which corresponds with a certain pony. If you were able to read the code, you could easily look for the pony you wanted without getting any doubles.

The first few waves had more random characters thrown in and were more focused on different gimmicks, like glitter-covered bodies and translucent features. After a few waves people got bored with the same moulds and characters being released over and over again. As a response, Hasbro released the Friendship is Magic collection in 2015. These sets were more about storytelling and contained several playsets themed after the *Friendship is Magic* series. Various unique moulds were also created alongside new characters. The blind bags waves were now also themed after the *Friendship is Magic* set released at that time.

There were many different blind bags released – some even of different species!

Bat-winged Pegasus with the Moonlight Chariot (front) and Princess Luna in packaging (back) from the Friendship is Magic Collection.

Several second wave blind bag ponies.

**Wave Two Blind Bag Characters**
**Release Year: 2011**

Blind bags are available in plenty of stores, are relatively cheap and there are no rare characters per set. However, there is one exception to this rule: the second wave of blind bags, which was only released in select European countries. While the release was sufficient for those European countries, plenty of collectors picked up on the exclusive release and wanted the figures too. At the start of the wave this didn't push up the price a lot, but with later *My Little Pony* blind bag waves, collectors started to realise that some characters from the second wave were never released again. These included popular side characters like Cheerilee, Daisy Dreams and glitter variants of Rarity, Applejack and Fluttershy. Cheerilee got another release in 2013, but Hasbro used another mould, which kept collectors interested in the original figure.

## Equestria Girls

In 2013 Hasbro released the Equestria Girls line as a spin-off of the *Friendship is Magic* series. The concept of the series is that there's a world where human counterparts of the ponies live, with the series focusing on the Mane Six and Sunset Shimmer, a pony who was banished to the human world by Princess Celestia. She eventually turned good and is now a student of Twilight Sparkle. This line of course led to Hasbro releasing actual dolls to compete with other doll-based brands, though they have been met with mixed reactions – the biggest complaints being that they have barely any articulation and do not look like the characters from the show. Still, the line was popular, with three films being released and several doll lines, including some exclusive dolls as well.

In 2015 Hasbro introduced the Equestria Girls Minis. These were smaller figures of the characters with sculpted hair instead of real hair. The Minis were more about the concept of storytelling, with playsets often being based on parts from the films so that children could recreate said scenes. So far the Minis have proven to be much more popular than the larger dolls, which eventually led to the discontinuation of the normal ones in 2016. 'Minis' was also removed from the packaging, which made it clear that the new dolls would be the primary release now for the line.

At the end of 2017 Hasbro decided to bring back the normal dolls to go with their brand-new YouTube series, but with a completely new look. The dolls were larger (about 11 inches) and had different, more realistically shaped bodies.

*Above left*: A scale comparison from left to right: Sunset Shimmer Mini, Sunset Shimmer Reboot Series Doll and Sour Sweet Friendship Games Doll.

*Above right*: Zecora Ponymania Equestria Girls Doll, released in 2014 under the Ponymania line.

*Above*: Rarity's Trendy Accessory Shop from the Equestria Girls Minis Mall Series.

*Left*: The Reboot Series Sunset Shimmer Equestria Girls Doll.

**Equestria Girls Singing Adagio Dazzle**
**Release year: 2014**
**Set: Rainbow Rocks Singing Dolls**

In pop culture it's common to see villains grow in popularity among the fans, and the same can be said for Adagio Dazzle. Around the *Equestria Girls: Rainbow Rocks* film, fans of the Equestria Girls series massively requested merchandise of Adagio Dazzle, but only a single full-sized doll was ever announced and released. But it isn't just any figure; the Adagio Dazzle doll is able to sing when you press on her arm.

Sadly, her release was plagued by shipping problems and limited store availability, which was worsened by the amount of people looking for her. This drove her price up to almost ten times the price of other singing dolls from the series. Even at the time of writing the Adagio Dazzle doll is still considerably more expensive than the Twilight Sparkle singing doll.

*Above left*: The Singing Adagio Dazzle Doll minus her wings.

*Above right*: A Mini version of Adagio Dazzle was released in 2016. (Pony provided by Celestiafan)

## Licensed Merchandise

**Funko Princess Celestia and Princess Luna Vinyl Figures**
**Release year: 2015**

Funko figures can be found in almost any toy store and video game shop. *My Little Pony* is no exclusion to their popularity, and over the years a lot of vinyl figures and smaller Funko Pop! figures have been released, some of them running for multiple years; yet, there were two ponies everyone was waiting for – the two main princesses, Celestia and Luna. With the ninth wave of Funko figures, it was finally time for the princesses to receive their vinyl counterpart. Both came in a larger box than the others vinyl ponies, because of the large mane, and collectors went wild for the amount of detail Funko put into the figures. However, there was a slight problem. The princesses were Hot Topic exclusives, much like the other ponies at the start of their release, but sales were so good that they quickly sold out. Another cause was the strike at the harbours, which caused the re-stock and nationwide release to halt. And, to add insult to injury, they never officially saw an aisle outside of Hot Topic. Once it became obvious that the figures were no longer available, the prices online went up incredibly, especially for buyers outside the United States. And, as if the two princesses weren't special enough, both received a 1:24 chase variant with a translucent and glitter-filled body, commonly being sold for twice as much as the regular princesses.

The regular variant of the Princess Luna Funko Vinyl Figure.

*Right*: The Glitter Chase variant of the Princess Luna Funko Vinyl Figure. (Pony provided by Celestiafan)

*Below*: The Glitter Chase variant of Princess Celestia in her box. (Pony provided by Celestiafan)

**Funko Hikari Rainbow Dash Statues**
**Release year: 2015**

The Hikari series is a side line of Funko that revolves around collectible figures with special finishes and a limited stock. For the *My Little Pony* series Funko chose a new Rainbow Dash design for the Hikari line of figures, announcing eight different designs of them in 2015, with the final version becoming available in 2016. Getting the complete set of eight variants was a huge challenge for fans of Funko and *My Little Pony*, mainly because each figure had a limited production run, going from 1,500 Glitter Noir versions being issued to only 250 Metallic figures.

Another problem for collectors was the fragmentation of places where each Hikari variant was available, ranging from a one-time sale at the New York Comic Con to a spread of figures across retailers and import businesses worldwide. The complete release run for the Rainbow Dash Hikari figures was as follows:

- Original: Various stores (700 pieces)
- Metallic: Entertainment Earth exclusive (250 pieces)
- Color Storm: BigBadToyStore exclusive (500 pieces)
- Glitter Storm: New York Comic Con 2015 Exclusive (600 pieces)
- Original Glitter: Various stores (1,000 pieces)
- Glitter Noir: Various stores (1,500 pieces)
- Glitterific: Modern Everyday exclusive (400 pieces)
- Gold Dust: Various stores (1,000 pieces)

The regular version of the Rainbow Dash Hikari was limited to 700 pieces. (Pony provided by Celestiafan)

**WeLoveFine Discord Flutter On Statue**

The growing relationship between Discord and Fluttershy was an interesting development in the *My Little Pony: Friendship is Magic* television series, and WeLoveFine used this interest as inspiration for their Discord Flutter On statue. First announced in 2014, it was due to be released in the second quarter of 2015 with a limited stock of 1,200 pieces. When the original release date wasn't met, panic arose, with the community asking themselves what happened to the statues. Shortly after WeLoveFine announced the devastating news that all 1,200 figures were either destroyed or damaged in the shipping process between the place of production and the WeLoveFine warehouse.

As a compensation people with a pre-order for the figure had the choice to either cancel their order for a full refund, get a larger refund in the form of store credit, or wait for a more expensive and durable re-production run of 1,400 pieces. Those that picked the last option also received an exclusive gold coin with the figure. In the final quarter of 2015 the statues were finally being shipped to those that had pre-ordered, and all remaining figures were made available in the WeLoveFine store at the start of 2016.

The Discord Flutter On statue. (Pony provided by Celestiafan)

The collectible coin that was offered for those who didn't cancel their order for the Discord statue. (Provided by Celestiafan)

# Special Thanks

We couldn't have completed this book without the help of people from the community who shot matching photos for the stories we have written. Therefore, we'd like to thank all people who have helped creating the visual part of this book:

Caitlin Beam; Celestiafan; Jessica M. Kriescher; K. Bollmeier; Krystal Dulce; Linda van Leeuwen (Moondancer paradise); Marina Strati; PirateParakeet; Satu (ebay.com/usr/satu567); Shelvesofwhimsy; Stephanie McPhie (CrystalSnowflake); and Victor A. Ramirez.

# About the Authors

Ilona and Ossie are two *My Little Pony* fans from the Netherlands. Ilona has a large collection of *My Little Pony* figures and merchandise from every generation and has been collecting them ever since her childhood during the second generation. Aside from a large collection she enjoys creating fan artwork of *My Little Pony* characters.

The authors have been running MLPmerch.com since 2014, a website about the latest *My Little Pony* merchandise news from around the world. This website has since evolved from a just a blog to a place where the collector community can find all relevant information on the latest releases and search a database of over 8,000 items from G4!

# Notes

1 Purple Pajama Press (2008), 'Bonnie Zacherle and My Little Pony from Dream to Reality'. Available at https://www.youtube.com/watch?v=TBRMukdQ8wg
2 Zacherle, et al. (1983) Toy animal US #D269986
3 My Pretty Pony – My Little Wiki. Available at: http://mylittlewiki.org/wiki/My_Pretty_Pony
4 Non-So-Soft Ponies – Ponyland Press. Available at: http://www.ponylandpress.com/europe/uk/nonsosoft.shtml
5 Horseshoe points was a loyalty program during Generation 1. Pony boxes and backcards contained points that you could cut out, collect and exchange for various (exclusive) mail order ponies.
6 Spanish Piggy Ponies – My Little Wiki. Available at: http://mylittlewiki.org/wiki/Spanish_Piggy_Ponies
7 Birthday – My Little Wiki. Available at: http://mylittlewiki.org/wiki/Birthday
8 1995: Mijn Kleine Pony – The My Little Pony Scrapbook. Available at: http://www.etherella.com/scrapbook2/1995.html
9 Breast Cancer Awareness Pony – My Little Wiki. Available at: http://mylittlewiki.org/wiki/Breast_Cancer_Awareness_Pony
10 Pony Project: White – Strawberry Reef. Available at: http://www.strawberryreef.com/Index/Name/ponyprojectwhite.html
11 Trolley – Strawberry Reef. Available at: http://www.strawberryreef.com/Index/Name/trolley.html